APEX PREDATORS
of the Amazon Rain Forest

Giant Otter

by Ellen Lawrence

Consultant:

Dr. Nicole Duplaix
Chair, IUCN/SSC Otter Specialist Group
Senior Instructor, Department of Fisheries and Wildlife
Oregon State University
Corvallis, Oregon

BEARPORT PUBLISHING

New York, New York

Credits

Cover, © ostill/Shutterstock and © Litvinova Olga/Shutterstock; 4, © Luciano Candisani/Minden Pictures/FLPA; 5, © Andrew M. Allport/Shutterstock; 6, © Cosmographics; 7, © Luiz Claudio Marigo/Nature Picture Library; 8, © Yan Hubert/Biosphoto; 9, © ostill/Shutterstock; 10T, © Christophe Courteau/Nature Picture Library; 10B, © Ondrej Prosicky/Shutterstock; 11, © Ben Cranke/Nature Picture Library; 12L, © Luciano Candisani/Minden Pictures/FLPA; 12R, © Dane Jorgensen/Shutterstock; 13, © Worawan Simaroj/Alamy; 14, © Claude Balcaen/Biosphoto/FLPA; 15, © Fabien Bruggmann & Bruno Fouillat/Biosphoto; 16–17, © Sean Crane/Minden Pictures/FLPA; 18T, © blickwinkel/Alamy; 18B, © Suzi Eszterhas/Minden Pictures/FLPA; 19, © Nicole Duplaix/Getty Images; 20, © blickwinkel/Alamy; 21, © blickwinkel/Alamy; 22, © Joe McDonald/Shutterstock; 23TL, © olgagorovenko/Shutterstock; 23TC, © JT Platt/Shutterstock; 23TR, © Steve Meese/Shutterstock; 23BL, © HamsterMan/Shutterstock; 23BC, © papillondream/Shutterstock; 23BR, © Konrad Wothe/Minden Pictures/FLPA.

Publisher: Kenn Goin
Senior Editor: Joyce Tavolacci
Creative Director: Spencer Brinker
Photo Researcher: Ruby Tuesday Books Ltd

Library of Congress Cataloging-in-Publication Data

Names: Lawrence, Ellen, 1967– author.
Title: Giant otter / by Ellen Lawrence.
Description: New York, New York : Bearport Publishing, [2017] | Series: Apex
    predators of the Amazon rain forest | Audience: Ages 5–8. | Includes
    bibliographical references and index.
Identifiers: LCCN 2016042360 (print) | LCCN 2016045162 (ebook) | ISBN
    9781684020348 (library) | ISBN 9781684020867 (ebook)
Subjects: LCSH: Otters—Juvenile literature.
Classification: LCC QL737.C25 L3868 2017 (print) | LCC QL737.C25 (ebook) |
    DDC 599.769—dc23
LC record available at https://lccn.loc.gov/2016042360

For more information, write to Bearport Publishing Company, Inc., 45 West 21st Street, Suite 3B, New York, New York 10010. Printed in the United States of America.

10 9 8 7 6 5 4 3 2 1

Contents

Gone Fishing!

A giant otter glides through a river in the Amazon **rain forest**.

Suddenly, it dives under the water.

Within seconds, the otter's sleek head bursts out of the river.

In the **predator**'s jaws is a large fish!

The otter grabs its wriggly **prey** with its front paws and munches on its breakfast.

a giant otter

A giant otter is an apex, or top, predator in its Amazon home. It's a highly skilled hunter with few enemies.

fish

paws

A Giant Otter's Home

Giant otters are large **mammals** that live in South America.

These big predators live on land and hunt for food in the water.

Many giant otters live in the Amazon rain forest.

There, they live alongside the rivers and streams that flow through the dense jungle.

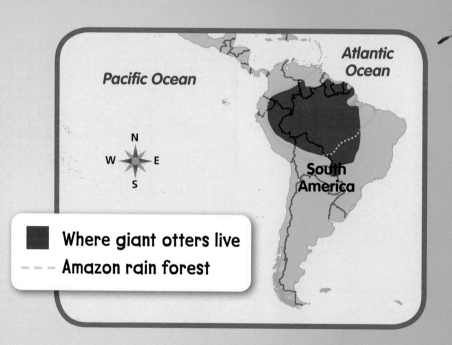

Atlantic Ocean

Pacific Ocean

South America

N
W E
S

■ Where giant otters live
- - - Amazon rain forest

Native people who live in the Amazon rain forest call the giant otter "river wolf." Why? It's a fierce predator— just like a wolf.

In what ways do you think a giant otter's body helps it move in water?

Super Swimmer

A giant otter's long, **streamlined** body helps it move quickly through the water.

As it swims, the otter uses its large, webbed paws as paddles.

To steer, it moves its thick, muscular tail from side to side.

The otter also has dense brown fur to keep it dry and warm when it's swimming.

webbed paw

River Hunter

When it's time to go hunting, a giant otter dives into the water.

It has long, sensitive whiskers that pick up tiny movements made by fish and other prey.

The hunter's excellent eyesight also helps it spot food.

Once it sees a fish, the otter zips through the water.

Finally, it grabs the fish with its sharp teeth.

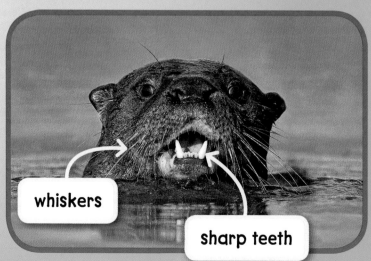

whiskers

sharp teeth

Giant otters eat fish such as piranhas and catfish. Sometimes, they also eat crabs and snakes.

Otter Camp

Giant river otters live in large family groups.

Each group includes the mother, father, their older pups, and young babies.

The family lives on a riverbank in an area known as a campsite.

There, the otters dig a home called a den with several rooms in it.

Around the den, they clear away plants to create a bare area for playing and sunbathing.

Each otter has unique white marks on its throat. How do you think the marks are useful to scientists?
(The answer is on page 24.)

a giant otter campsite

den entrance

bare area for playing

An otter family makes and uses several different campsites. They mark the edges of their camps with urine and piles of poop. This tells other otter families to keep out!

river

13

Helpless Babies

About once a year, the otter family gets some new members. How?

The mother and father otter **mate**.

Then the mother otter digs a birthing den away from the family's main camp.

About 70 days after mating, she gives birth to as many as five pups.

The tiny, newborn otters cannot see or walk.

a mother otter at the entrance to her birthing den

a giant otter pup

For the pups' first week, only the mother otter is allowed inside the birthing den. The other family members must wait until the babies are older to meet them.

Growing Up

The otter pups cuddle up to their mother and drink her milk.

The mother leaves the babies for only short periods of time to go hunting.

By the time they are four weeks old, the pups' eyes have opened.

At five weeks old, they start to walk around the den.

Soon, the babies are ready to explore outside.

mother otter

Sometimes, the family moves from one den to another. When they do this, the parent otters often carry the babies in their mouths.

Playful Pups

Once the otter pups are about eight weeks old, they start to learn how to swim.

The little otters follow their family into the river.

At first, they splash and struggle in the water.

After a few weeks, they can swim and dive with ease.

The pups also start to eat fish that their mother has caught.

an otter family swimming

A pup begs its mother for some fish.

Becoming Adults

By the time they are eight months old, the pups catch fish in the river with their family.

Soon, the pups' older brothers and sisters leave the family to begin their grown-up lives.

Next year, the otter parents will have more babies.

Then the growing pups will help care for their new brothers and sisters!

pups eating fish

Young otters live with their parents until they are about two years old. Then they leave home and find partners of their own.

21

Science Lab

Be a Giant Otter Scientist

Imagine you are a scientist who studies giant otters. Write a report all about a day in the life of an otter family.

Use the information in this book to help you. Draw pictures to include in your report, too.

When you are finished, present your report to friends and family.

Here are some words you can use in your report.

pups   campsite   swim   fish

den   webbed   predator

Read the questions below and think about the answers.

You can include some of the information from your answers in your report.

- *Where do giant otters live?*

- *How do giant otters find food?*

- *What skills do otter pups need to learn in order to survive?*

Science Words

mammals (MAM-uhlz) warm-blooded animals that drink their mother's milk as babies

mate (MAYT) to come together in order to have young

predator (PRED-uh-tur) an animal that hunts other animals for food

prey (PRAY) an animal that is hunted and eaten by another animal

rain forest (RAYN FOR-ist) a large area of land covered with trees and other plants where lots of rain falls

streamlined (STREEM-lined) having a shape that allows an animal to easily move through water

Index

Read More

Lawrence, Ellen. *North American River Otter (Swamp Things: Animal Life in a Wetland).* New York: Bearport (2017).

Leach, Michael. *Otter (Animal Neighbors).* New York: Rosen (2009).

Spilsbury, Louise. *Sea Otters (Living in the Wild: Sea Mammals).* Chicago: Heinemann-Raintree (2013).

Learn More Online

To learn more about giant otters, visit **www.bearportpublishing.com/ApexPredators**

About the Author

Ellen Lawrence lives in the United Kingdom. Her favorite books to write are those about nature and animals. In fact, the first book Ellen bought for herself, when she was six years old, was the story of a gorilla named Patty Cake that was born in New York's Central Park Zoo.

Answer for Page 12

When studying a giant otter family, scientists use the white markings on each otter's throat to identify different members of the family.